Readiness-Centred Change

How Systems Move When Conditions Support Them

Steve Barlow

Published by The Change Gym

ISBN: 978-0-9941530-2-9

CONTENTS

ACKNOWLEDGEMENTS

Books are never built alone. They take shape through conversations, questions, challenges, and the steady influence of people who help clarify the work.

To the leaders, teams, and organisations I've worked with over the years — thank you for your honesty, your curiosity, and your willingness to look beneath the surface of your own systems. Your experiences, insights, and struggles shaped the ideas in this book more than you may realise.

To the colleagues and collaborators who helped refine the thinking — thank you for the debates, the testing, the feedback, and the patience required to turn a set of ideas into a coherent architecture.

To the people closest to me — thank you for the support that made this work possible. Your steadiness, encouragement, and belief in the value of this project carried me through the long, quiet hours of writing.

And finally, to the readers who choose to engage with these ideas — thank you. Readiness is built through practice, and every leader who applies these concepts contributes to organisations that move with greater clarity, capability, and confidence.

This book is for you.

ABOUT THE AUTHOR

Steve Barlow is the founder of The Change Gym® and the architect of Readiness-Centred Change, a practical approach that helps leaders understand how systems behave under pressure and how to design the conditions that enable people to move with confidence.

With a PhD focused on change readiness, Steve has spent more than two decades working with organisations across sectors to build capability, strengthen alignment, and create environments where people can adapt reliably. His work integrates research, diagnostics, and hands-on practice, giving leaders a clear, structural way to interpret behaviour and shape the systems they lead.

Steve is the creator of the Readiness Engine, the Strategic Readiness Survey, and Redequip™, a suite of tools that help organisations diagnose conditions, design pathways, and develop sustainable capability. His thinking is grounded in the belief that readiness is not a program or an event — it is a way of working.

He lives on the Gold Coast in Australia, where he divides his time between consulting, writing, and woodworking — a craft that continues to shape his understanding of tension, alignment, sequence, and capability.

HOW TO USE THIS BOOK

This book is designed to be practical. It is not a theory text, a change management manual, or a collection of inspirational stories. It is a guide to understanding how systems behave under pressure and how leaders can shape the conditions that enable people to move with confidence.

You can read it straight through or use it as a reference. Either way, the structure is simple. This volume is the first in a three-book series. It introduces the core ideas in a clear, accessible way. The companion book explores the deeper architecture behind the framework for those who want to work with it at a technical or organisational level.

The Five Steps form the core

At the heart of the book are the Five Steps:

1. See the system clearly

2. Diagnose the conditions

3. Build the pathway

4. Support movement

5. Sustain capability

These steps form a developmental sequence. Each one builds on the one before it. You can apply them to any change effort, at any scale, in any organisation.

If you only read one part of the book, read the Five Steps.

The scenario shows the steps in action

After the Five Steps, you'll find a scenario that demonstrates how the steps play out inside a real organisational challenge. It's not a case study. It's a narrative designed to help you recognise the patterns in your own system.

Use it to see how the steps translate into practice.

The Map–Mechanism–Method chapter gives you the architecture

This chapter explains the organising logic behind readiness. It shows how the Five Steps fit together and why they work.

If you want the conceptual backbone — the mental model that ties everything together — this is where you'll find it.

The conclusion brings the ideas together

The final chapter reinforces the central message: readiness is not an event or a program. It is a way of working.

It shows how the Five Steps become a cycle that strengthens capability over time.

How to apply the ideas

You don't need to adopt everything at once. Start with the step that speaks most directly to your current challenge.

- If your system feels chaotic, start with Step 1.
- If behaviour doesn't make sense, start with Step 2.
- If progress keeps stalling, start with Step 3.
- If early movement is fragile, start with Step 4.
- If progress fades over time, start with Step 5.

Readiness is built through practice, not perfection.

A note on metaphors

Throughout the book, you'll see occasional references to woodworking. These metaphors are not decorative. They are structural — chosen because they reveal how systems behave:

- tension
- sequence
- alignment
- support
- capability
- drift

You don't need woodworking experience to understand them. They simply offer a clear way to see the logic of readiness.

Use this book as a lens, not a checklist

The Five Steps are not tasks to complete. They are a way of seeing, understanding, and shaping the system you lead.

Use them to:

- interpret behaviour
- diagnose conditions
- design pathways
- support movement
- sustain capability

And return to them whenever the system becomes harder to move than it should be.

INTRODUCTION — WHEN THE BOARD ISN'T FLAT

A board can look flat when it isn't. You run your hand across the surface and nothing feels out of place. The grain is straight. The edges look true. There's no obvious sign of trouble.

But when you lay a straightedge across it, the truth appears.

A slight twist. Subtle, but enough to throw every cut off. The board hasn't changed — only your understanding has.

It's a simple moment, but it reveals something important: you can't build anything reliable on a surface that only appears flat.

Organisations are no different.

On the surface, everything looks fine

The strategy is clear. The people are capable. The priorities make sense. The structures seem sound.

But the behaviour tells another story.

Deadlines drift. Teams hesitate. Communication loops without resolution. Initiatives lose momentum.

Leaders often respond by pushing harder or trying to motivate their way through the difficulty. But effort can't correct a structural distortion. Pressure can't flatten a twisted board. And no amount of enthusiasm will compensate for conditions that make movement difficult.

The system is shaping the behaviour.

Behaviour is not a mystery — it is a response

People don't resist change because they're unwilling. They don't hesitate because they lack commitment. They don't disengage because they're indifferent.

They behave in ways that make sense within the conditions they're navigating.

When clarity is thin, people become cautious. When capacity is stretched, they become overwhelmed. When signals contradict one another, they become confused. When agency is constrained, they become hesitant. When alignment weakens, they become reactive.

These aren't personal flaws. They're structural consequences.

Just as internal tension in timber reveals itself in the way a board refuses to lie flat, internal tension in a system reveals itself in the way people struggle to move — even when they want to.

Unreadiness is rarely intentional

Most organisations don't set out to make change difficult. They simply accumulate pressures and contradictions over time.

A new priority is added without removing an old one. A process lingers long after its purpose has faded. A team is stretched a little further, then further again. A signal from one part of the organisation contradicts another. A leader assumes clarity where none exists.

Individually, these things seem manageable. Together, they reshape the system.

Unreadiness is not a failure. It's a drift.

Readiness is not a mood — it is a condition

A readiness-centred system behaves differently.

It is clear. It is aligned. It is coherent under pressure. It gives people room to act and the support to succeed.

People don't need to be convinced to move. They move because the environment makes movement possible.

Readiness is not enthusiasm. It is not positivity. It is not "getting people on board."

Readiness is the structural capacity to adapt.

And it can be built.

Five steps make it possible

Every system — whether a workshop, a team, or an organisation — moves through five natural steps on the path to readiness:

1. See the system clearly
2. Diagnose the conditions
3. Build the pathway
4. Support movement
5. Sustain capability

These steps are practical, observable, and grounded in the physics of human behaviour under pressure. They describe how capability grows, how systems adapt, and how leaders can shape the environment so people can succeed.

This book is an invitation to look at your organisation the way a craftsperson looks at timber: with precision, with patience, and with an appreciation for the forces that shape it. Because once you see the twist in the board, you can finally begin the real work.

This book is the first in a three-part series. It introduces the core ideas in a clear, practical way. The companion volume explores the deeper architecture behind the Five Steps for those who want to work with the framework at a technical or organisational level.

The work begins with a shift in perspective. Before leaders can change a system, they must learn to see it. And that is where Step 1 starts.

STEP 1 — SEE THE SYSTEM CLEARLY

Most leaders begin by looking at people — their reactions, their attitudes, their behaviour. It's natural. Behaviour is visible. It's immediate. It's the part of the system that talks back. But behaviour is rarely the problem. It is almost always the consequence of something deeper: the conditions shaping how people make sense of the work.

Step 1 begins with a shift in perspective — from looking at people to seeing the system that is shaping them.

Emma had been watching her leadership team struggle with a simple decision that should have taken ten minutes. Instead, the conversation looped in circles. People repeated points. Others stayed quiet. No one committed. After forty minutes, the group agreed to "come back to it next week."

Walking out of the room, Emma felt the familiar frustration rising. *Why won't they just decide?* But as she replayed the meeting, something shifted. She realised no one actually had the information they needed. The priorities weren't clear. The risks weren't named. And the decision required cross-unit authority that no one in the room felt they had.

The behaviour made sense. The system didn't.

That was the moment she stopped looking at the people and started looking at the conditions shaping them.

There are moments in a workshop when the work slows, not because anything is wrong with the tools or the timber, but because something in the material doesn't match the picture in your head. You pick up a board that looks flat. It feels flat. Nothing about it suggests trouble.

But when you lay a straightedge across it, a twist reveals itself.

It's subtle — easy to miss if you're not looking for it — but enough to throw every cut out of alignment. The board hasn't changed. Your understanding has. And once you see the twist, you can't pretend it isn't there.

This is the essence of Step 1.

Most leaders are working with systems that look flat but aren't. The surface appears fine. The behaviour tells another story.

This is the work of Step 1.

Most leaders never reach this moment

Not because they lack intelligence or commitment, but because they are working from a model that no longer fits the conditions they're operating in. They're trying to interpret behaviour through assumptions inherited from a simpler time — when change was slower, complexity was lower, and systems were more predictable.

When the model is wrong, everything downstream becomes distorted.

Leaders misread hesitation as resistance. They treat overload as a mindset issue. They respond to symptoms instead of causes. They push harder, hoping effort will compensate for misalignment.

It never does.

Just as a fence that is out by half a millimetre will throw every cut off square, a mis-seen system will distort every interpretation of behaviour.

Behaviour is not a choice — it is a consequence

This is the first truth leaders must see clearly.

People behave in ways that make sense within the conditions they're navigating.

If the conditions support movement, people move. If the conditions suppress movement, people stall. If the conditions overwhelm capacity, people avoid. If the conditions contradict themselves, people become confused.

This isn't psychology. It's physics.

The Chisel and the Plane

Change is often treated as if it were the whole story — the tool, the action, the force that shapes the organisation. But change is only the **blade**. It cuts, slices, tears, bruises, or pares depending on how it is handled. A chisel can produce a clean, elegant surface, or it can gouge a piece of timber beyond repair. The blade itself doesn't determine the outcome. The *conditions* do.

A plane takes that same blade and places it inside a structure — a body, a sole, a mouth, a fixed angle, a controlled depth. The plane doesn't change the edge; it changes the **environment around the edge**. And that environment is what makes the cut predictable, safe, and effective. The plane turns raw force into controlled movement. It transforms risk into capability.

Change works the same way. Change is the blade. Readiness is the plane.

When organisations focus only on the blade — pushing harder, cutting deeper, applying more pressure — they get the same results you get when you drive a chisel into wood without support: tearout, resistance, damage, and frustration. But when they build the right environment around the change, the movement becomes smooth, controlled, and sustainable. The quality of the cut improves not because the blade changed, but because the **conditions** did.

Readiness doesn't replace change. It **enables** it. It turns change from force into craft.

In the workshop, you can often feel a problem before you can name it. A board that looks flat reveals a twist when you put a straightedge on it. A cut that should be clean tells you the fence is out. The system speaks through the behaviour.

Organisations do the same. Behaviour is the signal. Conditions are the cause.

Seeing clearly means seeing structurally

When you discover a twist in a board, you don't blame the timber. You adjust your understanding of the material. Wood moves because of the forces within it — tension, grain, moisture, and the way it was cut. The movement isn't personal. It's structural. You change how you work with it. You adapt your approach.

Leaders must do the same. Wood cannot learn. People can. That's why leaders must focus on the conditions shaping behaviour, not the character of the people displaying it.

Seeing clearly means looking past individual behaviour and focusing on the structural forces shaping it. It means recognising that people are not resisting the change — they are responding to the conditions.

It means understanding that capability is not a mindset — it is a function of environment, clarity, and strain.

Most importantly, it means recognising that behaviour is shaped by the system people are working in, as well as the capacity they bring with them. The system sets the conditions. People respond from the level of change fitness they've developed so far.

The Five Lenses of Clear Seeing

To see a system clearly, leaders must look through five lenses. These lenses reveal the architecture shaping behaviour and expose the hidden forces that determine whether a system is readiness-centred or unreadiness-centred.

1. The Lens of Reality

What is actually happening — not what should be happening, or what you hope is happening. In woodworking, reality is revealed by the cut. In organisations, reality is revealed by behaviour.

2. The Lens of Conditions

What pressures, constraints, and expectations are shaping behaviour? A board doesn't twist because it wants to. It twists because of the forces acting on it. People are no different.

3. The Lens of Capability

What can people reliably do under pressure? Not in theory. Not in calm conditions. In reality.

4. The Lens of Clarity

Do people understand the work, the expectations, and the environment? A cut made without a clear reference face is guesswork. Work done without clarity is the same.

5. The Lens of Alignment

Do the signals, structures, and expectations point in the same direction? If the fence and the bit aren't aligned, the cut will never be clean. If the system isn't aligned, behaviour will never be coherent.

These lenses reveal the architecture. They show leaders what is actually shaping behaviour.

Once you see the system clearly, everything changes

The frustration dissolves. The confusion lifts. The behaviour makes sense. The system becomes legible. Organisational behaviour becomes predictable once leaders understand the architecture.

And once you can see the architecture, you can diagnose it.

That is the work of Step 2.

STEP 2 — DIAGNOSE THE CONDITIONS

Once you see the twist in a board, the next question is obvious: *What caused it?*

Timber doesn't twist at random. It twists because of the forces acting on it — internal tension, uneven drying, grain direction, pressure, or the way the board was cut from the log. The twist is the symptom. The underlying forces are the conditions.

Organisations are the same.

Behaviour is the visible part. Conditions are the forces underneath.

Step 2 is about understanding those forces.

Mark had been frustrated with his operations team for weeks. Deadlines kept slipping. Updates were vague. Every meeting felt like a negotiation about what could be delivered rather than a clear plan for what would be done. He'd started to wonder whether the team had simply lost its edge.

But during a routine check-in, something caught his attention. One of the supervisors mentioned that two critical systems were running at half capacity because of a long-delayed upgrade. Another admitted they were covering three roles because vacancies hadn't been filled. A third quietly noted that priorities changed so often that no one knew which deadlines actually mattered.

Mark realised the team wasn't disengaged. They were overloaded, unclear, and stretched thin.

The behaviour made sense once the conditions came into view.

What looked like resistance was simply the system telling the truth about its own constraints.

Symptoms are easy to see. Conditions are not.

Leaders often focus on what they can observe:

- missed deadlines
- hesitation
- rework
- confusion
- disengagement
- slow progress
- inconsistent performance

These are symptoms — the organisational equivalent of a board that won't sit flat.

But symptoms don't tell you what's causing the distortion. They only tell you that *something* is causing it.

Diagnosis is the work of moving from the visible to the structural.

Conditions shape behaviour

Just as a plane only works when the sole, mouth, and angle are set correctly, organisations only move cleanly when the underlying conditions are aligned. Every system contains forces that influence how people respond to pressure, uncertainty, and change. These forces can support movement or suppress it. They can create clarity or confusion. They can build capability or drain it.

Conditions fall into a small number of predictable categories. Once you know what to look for, they become easier to see.

The Five Categories of Conditions

These categories form the backbone of diagnosis. They reveal the architecture shaping behaviour.

1. Pressure

Pressure is not inherently bad. Some pressure sharpens focus and accelerates learning. Too much pressure overwhelms capacity and triggers avoidance.

Pressure becomes a problem when:

- expectations exceed available capacity
- timelines compress without support
- multiple priorities compete
- strain accumulates faster than people can recover

Pressure shapes behaviour long before anyone names it.

2. Clarity

People cannot act confidently in fog.

Clarity is about:

- understanding the work
- knowing what matters most
- seeing how decisions are made

- recognising what "good" looks like

- knowing where the boundaries are

When clarity is thin, hesitation is rational.

3. Alignment

Alignment is the coherence of the system.

Signals, structures, and expectations must point in the same direction. When they don't, people receive mixed messages.

Misalignment shows up as:

- conflicting priorities

- leaders saying different things

- processes that contradict goals

- incentives that reward the wrong behaviour

A system cannot move cleanly when its components pull against each other.

4. Capacity

Capacity is not just workload. It is the ability to perform reliably under pressure.

Capacity includes:

- skills

- time

- energy

- attention

- emotional bandwidth

- Change Fitness

When capacity is stretched, behaviour becomes reactive. When capacity is supported, behaviour becomes adaptive.

5. Agency

Agency is the ability to act with confidence and autonomy.

People need:

- permission to move
- room to make decisions
- trust from leaders
- psychological safety
- a sense that their actions matter

When agency is constrained, people wait. When agency is supported, people step forward.

Diagnosis is the bridge between seeing and acting

In woodworking, once you understand the forces that shaped the timber, you know how to work with it. You adjust your approach. You choose the right tools. You change the sequence. You adapt to the material.

Leaders must do the same.

Diagnosis is not about blame. It is not about fault. It is not about finding who is "resisting."

Diagnosis is about understanding the forces shaping behaviour so you can design a pathway that works.

How diagnosis works in practice

Diagnosis begins with a simple question:

What conditions are shaping the behaviour I'm seeing?

From there, leaders look for patterns:

- Is pressure too high?
- Is clarity too low?
- Are signals misaligned?
- Is capacity stretched?
- Is agency constrained?

The goal is not to analyse everything. The goal is to identify the few conditions that matter most.

Because once you know the conditions, you know what must change.

Diagnosis reveals the pathway

A twisted board tells you how to plane it. A misaligned system tells you how to support it.

Diagnosis doesn't solve the problem. It tells you where to intervene and how to design the next step.

Diagnosis reveals the forces at play, but insight alone doesn't create movement. To help a system shift, leaders must design the conditions that make progress possible.

That is the work of Step 3.

STEP 3 — BUILD THE PATHWAY

Once you understand the forces shaping the timber, you can begin to work with it. A twisted board doesn't tell you what's wrong — it tells you what's needed. You don't fight the twist. You don't push harder. You don't hope it will behave differently.

You design the sequence that will bring it into alignment.

Organisations are no different.

Diagnosis reveals the conditions shaping behaviour. Step 3 is about designing the pathway that responds to those conditions.

This is the moment where readiness becomes practical.

Pathways are designed, not declared

Leaders often respond to unreadiness by announcing a plan, setting a deadline, or launching an initiative. But plans are not pathways. A pathway is not a list of tasks. It is a designed sequence of conditions that makes movement possible.

In woodworking, the order of operations matters. You flatten before you square. You square before you cut joinery. You cut joinery before you glue.

The sequence is not arbitrary. It is structural.

A good pathway follows the same logic.

Sofia had spent months trying to get her transformation program moving. Every time she met with her team, the list of issues seemed to grow. Communication gaps. Skill shortages. Legacy systems. Conflicting priorities. Cultural resistance. She kept adding actions, assigning tasks, and pushing for progress. But the harder she pushed, the more jammed the system became.

One morning, while reviewing yet another stalled workstream, she noticed something she had been too busy to see. Every initiative depended on something else that wasn't ready. Training required clarity. Clarity required decisions. Decisions required data. Data required access. Access required approvals. Everything was connected — but nothing was sequenced.

The problem wasn't effort. It was order.

Sofia realised she didn't need a bigger plan. She needed a pathway — a deliberate sequence of moves that would unlock the next step rather than overwhelm the system.

Once she mapped the dependencies, the noise settled. The work didn't get easier, but it finally made sense.

A pathway is built around three questions

Every effective pathway answers three architectural questions:

1. What must change first?

Not everything matters equally. Some conditions are foundational. Some are consequential. You don't fix a twisted board by sanding the surface. You start with the reference face.

2. What support will people need at each step?

Support is not generic. It must match the strain of the moment. Too much support creates dependency. Too little support creates overwhelm. The right support creates movement.

3. What sequence will make progress reliable?

Readiness grows through sequenced strain — not random effort, not heroic bursts, not motivational surges. A good pathway builds capability step by step.

The Architecture of a Good Pathway

A well-designed pathway has four structural elements. These elements are simple, but they are rarely done well.

1. A Clear Starting Point

You begin where the system actually is, not where you wish it were.

In woodworking, you don't start with the ideal dimensions. You start with the board in front of you. Skilled woodworkers know that the quality of the work is shaped long before the first cut — by selecting the pieces that will behave and designing the sequence around the material as it truly is.

Leaders must do the same.

2. A Small Number of Priorities

A pathway cannot carry everything. It must focus on the few conditions that matter most.

When everything is a priority, nothing is.

3. A Sequence That Builds Capability

Capability grows through:

- clarity

- practice

- feedback

- strain

- recovery

A good pathway introduces strain gradually, in a way that strengthens rather than overwhelms.

This is how change fitness develops.

4. Support Matched to Strain

Support is not a sign of weakness. It is a structural requirement.

In woodworking, jigs, fences, and guides are not shortcuts. They are supports that make precision possible.

In organisations, support does the same.

Pathways are built, not imposed

A pathway is not something leaders hand down. It is something they design *with* the system, not *for* it.

This means:

- listening to the people doing the work

- understanding their constraints

- recognising their capacity

- shaping conditions that enable success

- adjusting the sequence as the system responds

A pathway is a living design.

The goal of Step 3 is not to fix the system — it is to shape the environment so the system can move.

This is a crucial distinction.

Fixing is reactive. Designing is intentional. Fixing focuses on problems. Designing focuses on conditions. Fixing is about what's broken. Designing is about what's possible.

A pathway is a design for movement.

Once the pathway is built, people can begin to move

And this is where Step 4 begins.

Because a pathway, no matter how well-designed, does not create movement on its own. People create movement — when the environment supports them.

A well-designed pathway creates the potential for progress, but potential is not progress. People still need support as they take the first steps.

Step 4 is about supporting that movement in real time.

STEP 4 — SUPPORT MOVEMENT

A well-designed pathway creates the conditions for movement, but it does not create movement on its own. People still have to take the first step. And the first step is often the hardest.

In woodworking, even when the sequence is clear, the work still requires guidance. You use jigs, fences, stops, and reference faces not because you lack skill, but because precision depends on support. The right support makes the work predictable. The wrong support makes it risky.

Organisations are the same.

Step 4 is about providing the right support at the right moment, so people can move with confidence rather than hesitation.

Movement is fragile at the beginning

Early movement is easily disrupted. People are still learning the sequence. They're still interpreting the signals. They're still testing whether the environment is safe.

This is why early support matters so much.

Without support, people hesitate. With too much support, they disengage. With the wrong support, they become dependent.

The goal is not to carry people. The goal is to stabilise the environment so they can move under their own strength.

When the first signs of progress appeared, Daniel felt relieved. After months of stalled work, his team had finally begun trialling the new process. A few early wins came through. People seemed cautiously optimistic. For the first time in a long time, the project felt alive.

But within two weeks, the momentum faded. Updates slowed. Questions increased. A few team members quietly reverted to old habits. Daniel felt the frustration rising again. *Why can't they just stick with it?*

During a conversation with one of the frontline leads, the picture shifted. She explained that the team liked the new process — they just weren't sure it would last. They'd seen too many initiatives start strong and then disappear when pressure increased or priorities changed. They weren't resisting. They were waiting to see whether this one would hold.

The behaviour made sense. The system hadn't earned their confidence yet.

Daniel realised early movement wasn't something to celebrate and walk away from. It was something to protect. The team didn't need more motivation. They needed reassurance, clarity, and visible support while the new way of working found its footing.

Once he provided that support — answering questions quickly, removing small obstacles, reinforcing priorities — the movement stabilised. What had looked like resistance was simply the system testing whether the pathway was real.

Support is structural, not emotional

Support is not about encouragement or motivation. It is about shaping the environment so that movement is:

- clear
- safe
- predictable
- repeatable

In woodworking, support is built into the setup. In organisations, support is built into the conditions.

Support shows up as:

- clarity at the moment of action
- access to guidance when needed
- space to practise without penalty
- feedback that strengthens capability
- leaders who remove friction rather than add pressure

Support is not a pep talk. It is a design choice.

The Four Forms of Support

Every system needs four forms of support to enable movement. These are simple, but they are rarely provided with intention.

1. Directional Support

People need to know:

- what to do next
- what "good" looks like

- how to interpret the signals around them

Directional support reduces hesitation. It gives people a clear reference face.

2. Structural Support

This is the scaffolding that makes movement possible:

- tools

- processes

- templates

- checklists

- workflows

- access to expertise

Structural support reduces friction. It makes the work stable.

3. Relational Support

People need to feel:

- trusted

- backed

- safe to try

- safe to learn

- safe to ask for help

Relational support reduces fear. It creates the psychological space for movement.

4. Developmental Support

This is the support that builds capability over time:

- feedback

- reflection

- practice

- coaching

- opportunities to stretch

- recovery

Developmental support strengthens change fitness. It turns movement into growth.

Support must match the strain

Support is not generic. It must be calibrated to the moment.

Too much support removes challenge. Too little support creates overwhelm. The right support creates capability.

In woodworking, you remove jigs as your skill grows. In organisations, you remove support as capability strengthens.

Support is temporary. Capability is permanent.

Leaders support movement by shaping the environment, not by pushing people

Pushing creates compliance. Support creates capability.

Pushing creates shortterm movement. Support creates sustainable movement.

Pushing relies on pressure. Support relies on design.

Leaders who support movement:

- remove friction
- clarify expectations
- provide guidance
- create space for practice
- protect early progress
- adjust conditions as the system responds

They don't push harder. They shape the environment.

Movement reveals what the system needs next

As people begin to move, new information emerges:

- where the friction is
- where the gaps are
- where the strain is too high
- where the support is too low
- where the sequence needs adjusting

Movement is diagnostic. It tells you how the system is responding.

This is why Step 4 and Step 5 are connected. Step 4 supports movement.

As movement begins, capability starts to grow — but early progress is fragile. Without reinforcement, systems drift back to old patterns.

Step 5 focuses on sustaining what has been built.

STEP 5 — SUSTAIN CAPABILITY

When a piece of timber has been brought into alignment, the work isn't finished. You still need to stabilise it. Freshly flattened faces can move again if the internal tensions aren't balanced. A joint that fits perfectly today can open tomorrow if the structure around it isn't supported.

Capability is the same.

Movement is the beginning. Sustaining it is the work that follows.

Step 5 is about embedding capability into the system so it becomes reliable under pressure, not just possible in ideal conditions.

Capability is not an event — it is a pattern

A team can perform well for a week. A leader can show clarity for a moment. A system can behave coherently for a short burst.

But sustained capability is different. It is the ability to perform reliably, repeatedly, and predictably — even when conditions tighten.

This is the longgrain strength of readiness.

Lena had seen her team make real progress over the past few months. The new workflow was in place. The early stumbles had settled. People were moving with more confidence. For the first time in years, the work felt coherent.

But as the next quarter began, she noticed something unsettling. A few shortcuts crept back in. Some teams stopped using the new templates. A couple of leaders reverted to old reporting habits. Nothing dramatic — just small deviations that, if left unchecked, would eventually pull the system back to where it started.

Her first instinct was to push harder. More reminders. More check-ins. More pressure.

But during a conversation with one of her senior analysts, she realised something important. The team wasn't slipping because they disagreed with the new way of working. They were slipping because they hadn't yet built the muscle memory to sustain it. The new workflow made sense — but it wasn't second nature.

The behaviour made sense. The capability wasn't fully formed.

Lena shifted her approach. Instead of pushing, she created space for practice. She built short, regular routines that reinforced the new habits. She encouraged teams to review their own work, spot their own drift, and correct it early. She made the new way of working visible, discussable, and repeatable.

Slowly, the system stabilised. People didn't just follow the new workflow — they owned it. The capability became part of how the organisation worked, not something held together by leadership effort.

What had looked like backsliding was simply the system asking for practice.

Systems drift without reinforcement

Every system has a natural tendency to drift back toward familiar patterns. Not because people are unwilling, but because:

- pressure returns

- clarity erodes

- alignment loosens

- habits reassert themselves

- old constraints reappear

- new demands accumulate

Without reinforcement, the system slowly bends back toward unreadiness.

Sustaining capability is the work of countering that drift.

The Three Anchors of Sustained Capability

There are three structural anchors that keep capability stable over time. These anchors are simple, but they require intention.

1. Reinforce the conditions that created movement

When movement begins, it's tempting to shift focus to the next priority. But early movement is fragile. It needs reinforcement.

This means:

- keeping clarity high

- protecting alignment

- maintaining realistic pressure

- ensuring capacity isn't stretched

- preserving agency

You don't remove the supports the moment the board lies flat. You let the structure settle.

2. Build habits that make capability automatic

Capability becomes sustainable when it becomes habitual.

Habits form through:

- repetition
- reflection
- feedback
- small adjustments
- consistent expectations

In woodworking, muscle memory develops through repeated cuts, not occasional ones. In organisations, capability develops through repeated practice, not one-off efforts.

Habits turn movement into reliability.

3. Strengthen change fitness over time

Change fitness is developmental. It grows through:

- exposure to manageable strain
- opportunities to practise
- cycles of effort and recovery
- learning from real work
- increasing levels of challenge

Sustaining capability means designing the environment so people continue to grow, not just cope.

This is how readiness becomes part of the system's identity.

Sustaining capability requires leadership attention, not leadership pressure

Leaders often try to sustain progress by pushing harder. But pressure doesn't sustain capability — it erodes it.

What sustains capability is:

- consistency
- clarity
- reinforcement
- reflection
- small course corrections
- attention to early signs of drift

Leaders don't hold the system up. They shape the environment so the system holds itself up.

Sustaining capability is the quiet work that makes readiness real

It's not dramatic. It's not loud. It doesn't produce instant wins.

But it is the work that:

- prevents regression
- stabilises progress
- strengthens confidence
- builds resilience
- embeds new patterns
- prepares the system for the next challenge

This is the moment where readiness stops being an aspiration and becomes a property of the system.

The Five Steps form a cycle, not a line

Once capability is sustained, the system is ready for the next level of challenge. And the cycle begins again:

1. See the system clearly

2. Diagnose the conditions

3. Build the pathway

4. Support movement

5. Sustain capability

Readiness is not a destination. It is a way of working.

And when leaders adopt this way of working, organisations become capable of adapting — not occasionally, but consistently.

The Five Steps form a clear developmental sequence, but they become most powerful when seen in practice. The following scenario shows how the steps play out inside a real organisational challenge.

THE SCENARIO — WHEN A STRATEGY STALLS

A Tale of Two Systems

Every organisation tells a story through its behaviour. Not the story written in strategy documents or spoken in town halls, but the story revealed in the way people act when pressure rises, when priorities collide, or when clarity is thin. Behaviour is the system speaking.

By this point in the book, you've seen the Five Steps of readiness. You've seen how leaders shift from looking at people to seeing the conditions shaping them. You've seen how pathways are designed, how movement is supported, and how capability is sustained.

But readiness is not theory. It is something you can see.

This chapter brings the Five Steps to life through two contrasting scenarios. Both organisations face similar challenges. Both have smart people, committed leaders, and important work to deliver. But the way their systems behave — and the way their leaders respond — could not be more different.

The difference is not personality. It is not culture. It is not motivation. It is readiness.

These scenarios show how the same pressures can produce entirely different outcomes depending on the conditions, the sequence, and the support surrounding the work. They also show how the

Map–Mechanism–Method lens helps leaders see what is actually happening beneath the surface.

What follows is not fiction. It is a composite of patterns seen across hundreds of organisations — the predictable ways systems behave when they are ready, and when they are not.

Let's begin.

The organisation wasn't in crisis. It wasn't dysfunctional. It wasn't chaotic.

It was simply stuck.

A new strategic priority had been launched six months earlier — a shift toward more integrated service delivery across three business units. The logic was sound. The market demanded it. The executive team agreed it was essential.

Yet progress was slow, inconsistent, and fragile.

Teams were doing "pieces" of the work. Leaders were talking about the strategy, but not acting on it. Deadlines drifted. Meetings filled with updates rather than decisions. Everyone agreed the strategy mattered — but nothing was moving at the pace required.

THE FIRST SCENARIO — WHEN A STRATEGY STALLS

1. The Situation

Emma, the executive responsible for the rollout, was frustrated. She had a capable team. She had a clear plan. She had communicated the strategy repeatedly.

But the system wasn't responding.

People weren't resisting. They weren't disengaged. They weren't confused.

They were simply… not moving.

Emma's instinct was to push harder — more meetings, more reminders, more pressure. But she'd done that before, and it had never worked for long.

This time, she paused.

2. The Symptoms

The symptoms were familiar:

- teams waiting for direction
- decisions bouncing between leaders
- inconsistent interpretations of priorities
- rework caused by misalignment
- slow progress on foundational tasks
- pockets of momentum that faded quickly

These were the organisational equivalent of a board that won't sit flat. Visible. Frustrating. But not diagnostic.

Emma realised she was looking at symptoms, not causes.

3. Step 1 — See the System Clearly

Emma shifted her attention from the people to the system.

Instead of asking, *"Why won't they move?"* she asked, *"What is shaping this behaviour?"*

She looked at the work, not the intentions. She looked at the patterns, not the moments. She looked at the system, not the individuals.

And when she did, the picture changed.

The behaviour made sense. The system didn't.

This was her "twisted board" moment — the realisation that the surface looked fine, but the underlying structure wasn't supporting movement.

4. Step 2 — Diagnose the Conditions

Once she saw the system clearly, the conditions revealed themselves.

Pressure
Teams were carrying legacy priorities that hadn't been retired. The new strategy was added on top of existing workloads.

Clarity

The strategy was clear at the executive level, but vague at the operational level. Teams didn't know what "integrated service delivery" meant in practice.

Alignment

Different leaders were emphasising different aspects of the strategy. Signals were inconsistent.

Capacity

Some teams had the skills required. Others didn't — but no one had named it.

Agency

People were waiting for permission to make cross-unit decisions. The system had trained them to stay in their lane.

None of this was about motivation. None of it was about attitude. All of it was structural.

Emma now understood why the system wasn't moving.

5. Step 3 — Build the Pathway

With the conditions clear, Emma designed a pathway.

Not a plan. Not a list of tasks. A sequence.

She identified three foundational moves:

1. Retire legacy priorities to reduce pressure.

2. Define what integrated service delivery looks like in concrete terms.

3. Create a cross-unit decision forum to give people agency.

These were the reference faces — the structural elements that would make everything else possible.

She didn't try to fix everything. She focused on the few conditions
that mattered most.

The pathway was simple, but it was structural.

6. Step 4 — Support Movement

As the pathway rolled out, early movement appeared.

Teams began using the new decision forum. Leaders started aligning
their messages. Workload pressure eased as old priorities were retired.

But early movement is fragile.

Emma provided support matched to the strain:

- **Directional support** — clear next steps
- **Structural support** — templates, workflows, shared tools
- **Relational support** — leaders backing decisions publicly
- **Developmental support** — coaching for teams new to
  cross-unit work

She didn't push harder. She shaped the environment.

Movement stabilised.

7. Step 5 — Sustain Capability

As capability grew, Emma focused on reinforcement.

She kept clarity high. She protected alignment. She ensured
the decision forum stayed active. She created space for teams to
reflect on what was working. She gradually reduced support as
capability strengthened.

The system began to hold itself up.

What had once been a fragile shift became a reliable pattern.

8. The Outcome

The organisation didn't transform overnight. It didn't become perfect. It didn't eliminate all friction.

But it became capable of moving — consistently, predictably, and under pressure.

The strategy that had stalled for six months began to take shape. Teams collaborated more easily. Decisions flowed. Progress became visible. Confidence grew.

The system was no longer stuck. It was ready.

THE CONTRASTING SCENARIO — WHEN A STRATEGY MOVES

The organisation faced the same strategic challenge: a shift toward more integrated service delivery across three business units. The logic was sound. The market demanded it. The executive team agreed it was essential.

But this organisation behaved differently.

Progress wasn't perfect, but it was steady. Teams were moving. Decisions were being made. Momentum was visible.

This is where the contrasting scenario begins.

1. The Situation

Amira, the executive responsible for the rollout, wasn't pushing the strategy uphill. She wasn't chasing updates. She wasn't trying to generate momentum through pressure.

The system was already moving.

Not quickly. Not flawlessly. But coherently.

People weren't waiting for direction. They were seeking it. Leaders weren't protecting their units. They were aligning them. Teams weren't confused. They were experimenting.

The difference wasn't enthusiasm. It was readiness.

2. The Signals

The signals were subtle but unmistakable:

- teams clarifying assumptions before starting work
- decisions being made at the right level
- leaders reinforcing the same priorities
- cross-unit conversations happening early, not late
- issues being surfaced before they became problems
- small wins accumulating into visible progress

These were the organisational equivalent of a board that sits flat on the bench — not because it is perfect, but because the forces around it are balanced.

Amira recognised these signals immediately. The system wasn't just behaving well. It was behaving predictably.

3. Step 1 — See the System Clearly

Amira didn't begin by looking at people. She began by looking at the system.

She mapped the work, the dependencies, the decision points, and the pressure points. She looked for patterns, not moments. She looked for conditions, not attitudes.

What she saw was a system that made sense.

The behaviour aligned with the environment. The environment aligned with the strategy.

This was her "straight board" moment — the realisation that the structure was supporting the work rather than distorting it.

4. Step 2 — Diagnose the Conditions

The conditions were not perfect, but they were aligned.

Pressure
Legacy priorities had been retired before the strategy launched. People had space to move.

Clarity
The executive team had defined what integrated service delivery meant in concrete, operational terms.

Alignment
Leaders were sending consistent signals. No mixed messages. No competing interpretations.

Capacity
Teams had been given time and support to build the skills required for cross-unit work.

Agency
Decision rights were clear. People knew what they could decide — and they used that authority.

None of this happened by accident. All of it was structural.

Amira understood why the system was moving.

5. Step 3 — Build the Pathway

With the conditions aligned, Amira designed a pathway that amplified the movement already underway.

She focused on three enabling moves:

1. A shared planning rhythm across the three business units.
2. A simple integration checklist used before any major decision.
3. A weekly cross-unit standup to surface issues early.

These weren't tasks. They were structural supports — the reference faces that kept the work aligned.

The pathway didn't create movement. It channelled it.

6. Step 4 — Support Movement

As teams began working in new ways, Amira provided support matched to the strain.

- **Directional support** — reinforcing the next step, not the whole journey
- **Structural support** — shared tools that made integration easier
- **Relational support** — leaders backing cross-unit decisions publicly
- **Developmental support** — coaching as new challenges emerged

She didn't hover. She didn't push. She stabilised.

Movement didn't just continue — it strengthened.

7. Step 5 — Sustain Capability

As capability grew, Amira shifted her focus to reinforcement.

She protected the planning rhythm. She kept the integration checklist alive. She ensured the cross-unit standup remained a place for real issues, not polite updates. She created space for teams to reflect, refine, and improve.

Support decreased as capability increased. The system began to hold itself up.

What had started as a strategic shift became a reliable pattern.

8. The Outcome

The organisation didn't become perfect. It didn't eliminate friction. It didn't avoid every setback.

But it became capable of moving — consistently, predictably, and under pressure.

The strategy didn't stall. It took shape.

Teams collaborated naturally. Decisions flowed. Progress was visible. Confidence grew.

The system wasn't just aligned. It was ready.

What These Scenarios Reveal

Both organisations faced the same strategic challenge. Both had capable people, committed leaders, and a clear need to move. Yet their systems behaved in completely different ways.

One stalled. One moved.

The difference wasn't motivation. It wasn't culture. It wasn't personality. It was the underlying architecture.

In the first organisation, the conditions weren't aligned. Pressure was high, clarity was thin, agency was limited, and the sequence of work wasn't designed. The system behaved logically — it protected itself from overload.

In the second organisation, the conditions supported movement. Pressure was managed, clarity was concrete, alignment was real, and the sequence was deliberate. The system behaved logically — it moved.

Readiness is not mysterious. It is structural.

These scenarios show how behaviour emerges from the interaction between the **Map** (the terrain), the **Mechanism** (the forces shaping behaviour), and the **Method** (the sequence of moves that create movement). When these three elements are aligned, systems move. When they are not, systems stall.

The next chapter introduces this architecture — the Map, the Mechanism, and the Method — and shows how leaders can use it to understand, diagnose, and shape the systems they lead.

THE MAP, THE MECHANISM, AND THE METHOD

Every leader knows the feeling of standing inside a complex system and trying to make sense of what's happening. The work is moving, but not in the way you expected. People are responding, but not in the way you hoped. The system is behaving, but not in the way you designed.

This is where most change efforts falter — not because leaders lack intelligence or commitment, but because they lack a clear organising logic for understanding what they're seeing.

Readiness provides that logic.

At the heart of readiness is a simple, structural flow:

The Map → The Mechanism → The Method

This flow is not a model to memorise. It is a way of thinking — a way of making sense of behaviour, conditions, and capability.

1. The Map — What You're Looking At

The Map is your understanding of the system.

It answers the question: **What is the terrain?**

The Map includes:

- the work

- the pressures

- the constraints

- the expectations

- the relationships

- the history

- the patterns of behaviour

Without a clear map, leaders misinterpret what they see. They mistake symptoms for causes. They assume behaviour is personal rather than structural. They respond to moments instead of patterns.

The Map is Step 1: *see the system clearly*. It is the moment when the twist in the board becomes visible.

2. The Mechanism — What's Shaping the Behaviour

Once you can see the system, the next question is:

What forces are shaping what I'm seeing?

This is the Mechanism — the structural forces that produce behaviour.

In organisations, these forces show up as:

- pressure

- clarity

- alignment

- capacity

- agency

These are not abstract ideas. They are the real, tangible conditions that shape how people respond to uncertainty, strain, and change.

The Mechanism is Step 2: *diagnose the conditions.* It is the moment when you understand why the board is twisted.

3. The Method — What You Do Next

Once you understand the forces shaping behaviour, the next question becomes:

How do I design the environment so the system can move?

This is the Method — the practical sequence of actions that build readiness.

The Method is expressed through:

- building the pathway
- supporting movement
- sustaining capability

These are Steps 3, 4, and 5.

The Method is not a plan. It is not a checklist. It is not a set of instructions.

It is a design process — a way of shaping conditions so people can move with confidence and capability.

It is the moment when you choose the sequence that brings the timber into alignment.

Why This Flow Matters

Most change efforts fail because leaders jump straight to the Method. They start with action. They start with solutions. They start with plans.

But without the Map, the Method is misdirected. Without the Mechanism, the Method is misaligned.

The Map tells you what you're looking at. The Mechanism tells you what's shaping it. The Method tells you what to do next.

This flow is the architecture of readiness.

How the Flow Works in Practice

In the Scenario chapter, Emma followed this flow intuitively:

- She mapped the system — seeing patterns rather than moments.

- She identified the mechanism — the conditions shaping behaviour.

- She applied the method — designing a pathway, supporting movement, and sustaining capability.

This is how readiness becomes practical. This is how leaders move from frustration to clarity. This is how systems shift from stuck to moving.

The Map–Mechanism–Method
Flow Is Not a Framework

It is a way of thinking.

It gives leaders:

- a way to interpret behaviour

- a way to understand conditions

- a way to design movement

- a way to build capability

- a way to sustain progress

It is the quiet architecture behind every successful change effort.

And once leaders adopt this way of thinking, they stop reacting to behaviour and start shaping the environment that produces it.

Understanding the architecture is essential, but leaders also need a quick way to recognise what they're looking at in their own system. The following matrix offers a simple diagnostic lens — a way to identify the current state of readiness so you know where to begin in the Five Steps.

READINESS STATE MATRIX

A quick diagnostic for understanding
where your organisation stands

This matrix gives leaders a fast way to interpret the current state of readiness in their system. It is not a scorecard. It is a lens — a way to understand the conditions shaping behaviour and the level of capability the system can reliably demonstrate.

Use it to identify where you are, not to judge where you "should" be.

THE MATRIX

Readiness State	What You See	What It Means Structurally	Implication for Leaders
1. Unready	Hesitation, confusion, inconsistent behaviour, stalled progress	Conditions misaligned: pressure too high, clarity too low, alignment fractured, capacity stretched, agency constrained	Do not push. Begin at Step 1 and Step 2. The system cannot move yet.
2. Partially Ready	Some movement, but fragile and inconsistent; pockets of progress	Some conditions are supportive, others are working against movement	Focus on Step 2 and Step 3. Fix the few conditions that matter most.
3. Conditionally Ready	Movement occurs when pressure is low or support is high; progress collapses under strain	Capability exists but is not stable; conditions are uneven	Step 3 and Step 4 are essential. Build a pathway and support early movement.
4. Ready Enough to Move	Consistent progress, growing confidence, predictable behaviour	Conditions are aligned enough for reliable movement; capability is developing	Step 4 and Step 5. Support movement and reinforce capability.

Readiness State	What You See	What It Means Structurally	Implication for Leaders
5. Fully Ready	Reliable performance under pressure; adaptive behaviour; sustained progress	Conditions are aligned and capability is stable; the system holds itself up	Step 5. Sustain capability and prepare for the next cycle.

HOW TO USE THE MATRIX IN PRACTICE

This matrix is not a replacement for the Five Steps. It is a snapshot — a way to quickly understand the system's current state so you know where to begin.

- If you're in **State 1 or 2**, start with seeing and diagnosing.
- If you're in **State 3**, focus on pathway design and early support.
- If you're in **State 4**, reinforce and stabilise.
- If you're in **State 5**, sustain and prepare for the next cycle.

The matrix helps leaders avoid the most common mistake in change: **trying to move a system that is not ready to move.**

With the architecture clear, the final step is to bring the ideas together. The conclusion shows how readiness becomes a way of working, not a one-off effort.

CONCLUSION — A WAY OF WORKING

Every organisation faces moments when the work becomes harder than it should be. Not because people lack commitment, but because the system is shaping behaviour in ways no one intended. When this happens, leaders often push harder, communicate more, or demand greater effort. But effort alone cannot overcome structural forces.

Readiness offers a different path.

It gives leaders a way to see the system clearly, understand the forces shaping behaviour, and design the conditions that enable people to move with confidence. It replaces frustration with clarity, pressure with structure, and reactive effort with intentional design.

Readiness is not a program. It is not a toolkit. It is not a set of motivational techniques.

It is a way of working.

Readiness begins with how you see

When you stop interpreting behaviour as personal and start seeing it as structural, everything changes. Patterns become visible. Causes become clearer. The system becomes understandable.

This shift in perspective is the foundation of readiness.

Readiness grows through design

Once you understand the conditions shaping behaviour, you can design a pathway that makes movement possible. Not a plan. Not a list of tasks. A sequence.

A sequence that reduces unnecessary pressure, increases clarity, strengthens alignment, builds capacity, and restores agency.

This is the work of leadership — not pushing people, but shaping the environment so they can move.

Readiness becomes real through practice

Movement is fragile at the beginning. It needs support. It needs reinforcement. It needs leaders who understand that capability grows through manageable strain, not heroic effort.

As capability strengthens, the system becomes more stable. Patterns become reliable. Confidence grows.

This is how readiness becomes part of the organisation's identity.

Readiness is sustained through attention

Systems drift. Clarity erodes. Pressure accumulates. Alignment loosens.

Sustaining capability requires leaders who pay attention to the early signs of drift and reinforce the conditions that support movement. This is not dramatic work. It is quiet, deliberate, and deeply practical.

It is the work that makes progress durable.

Readiness is a cycle, not a destination

The Five Steps form a loop:

1. See the system clearly

2. Diagnose the conditions

3. Build the pathway

4. Support movement

5. Sustain capability

And then the cycle begins again.

Each time you move through the cycle, the system becomes more capable. Each time, people become more confident. Each time, readiness becomes more deeply embedded.

This is how organisations develop the ability to adapt — not occasionally, but consistently.

The work continues

Change will always be the blade. Readiness is the plane that makes the cut clean. When leaders shape the environment, movement becomes possible and capability becomes sustainable. No organisation reaches a point where readiness is complete. Conditions shift. Priorities evolve. Pressure returns.

But leaders who practise readiness are never unprepared. They know how to see. They know how to diagnose. They know how to design. They know how to support. They know how to sustain.

They know how to lead systems that can move.

That is the real work of change — not pushing harder, but shaping the conditions that allow people to act with clarity, confidence, and agency.

The Five Steps give you the pathway. Beneath them sits a deeper architecture — the forces that shape behaviour, the conditions that strengthen capability, and the structures that determine how systems respond under pressure.

Readiness is built through practice, attention, and intention. And it begins every time a leader chooses to look beyond behaviour and see the system that is shaping it.

The work is ongoing. But now, you know where to begin.

Readiness-Centred Change explains how leaders design the underlying architecture that makes adaptive behaviour possible. While Book 1 focuses on how systems move when conditions support them, this volume goes deeper into the structural forces that shape behaviour. It shows leaders how to design the conditions, constraints, and mechanisms that create readiness as an emergent property of the system. Using the map–mechanism–method framework, the book provides a clear way to see how systems function under pressure and how to build the architecture that supports capability, agency, and capacity. The tone is structural, precise, and practical, aimed at leaders who want to design environments where meaningful change becomes possible.